No Sweat Projects
Thumbs Up
Science

by Jess Brallier
Illustrated by Bob Staake

Published by Planet Dexter, a division of Penguin Putnam Books for Young Readers,
New York.
PLANET DEXTER and the PLANET DEXTER logo are registered trademarks of
Penguin Putnam Inc.
Printed in the United States. Published simultaneously in Canada.

Library of Congress Cataloging-in Publication Data is available.

ISBN 0-448-44085-7 (pb.) A B C D E F G H I J
ISBN 0-448-44094-6 (GB) A B C D E F G H I J

Many of the designations used by manufacturers and sellers to distinguish their
products are claimed as trademarks. Where those designations appear in this book
and Planet Dexter was aware of a trademark claim, the designations have been
printed with initial capital letters.

And Now a Message from Our Corporate Lawyer:

"Neither the Publisher nor the Author shall be liable for any damage
that may be caused or sustained as a result of conducting any of the
activities in this book without specifically following instructions, conducting the activities without proper supervision, or ignoring the
cautions contained in the book."

A Thumber's Guide

Introduction

So why does this book exist?

- Need to do a science report or project?
- Looking for a subject that's really interesting and fun?
- Searching for an idea that'll impress your teacher and amaze your classmates?
- Need a subject that you know really well?
- Hoping to spend very little, or no, money?
- Are you running out of time?

This book is the answer to all those questions.

What this book will not do is your school work. This book gives you ideas, illustrations you can copy, and it even helps get you started on your **research**. But **you** have to do **your** own work.

Hello!
Research is gathering information for your project.

So? What kind of science project do you need to do?

As a student, you may be told to:

or Write a two-page or a five-page report.

or Present a three-minute oral report to the class.

Write a three-page report *and* present a three-minute oral report to the class.

or

Write a three-page report *and* make a poster to be placed in the school cafeteria for parents' evening.

or

Work with three classmates to do a written report *and* present something extra before the whole class.

or

Present an oral report and use stuff like handouts, posters, etc.

Luckily, Thumbs Up Science is perfect for any of these. As you use this book, it will tell you how ideas can be used for different types of reports and projects.

But Why the Thumb?

There are many good reasons to make the thumb the subject of your science project.

For example:

Comfort

You know your thumb. You were probably sucking on it even before you were born. It's a life-long buddy.

Cost

Your thumb's free. You don't need to go out and buy one.

Everybody in class has one

No need to buy, copy, or make 20 or 30 thumbs to hand out to your classmates. Hey, they'll know what you're talking about!

Parents

The thumb is such a simple project that you won't have to bug your parents. (Bugging parents is best saved for when you need new toys or clothes.)

You can't forget it

Ever work really hard on something and then forget to bring it to school? Don't you hate that?! No need to worry when your subject is "The Thumb"—it goes wherever you go.

The thumb makes for a great science project because it is so important.

What is one of the things that sets humans apart from all other animals? Think about it. Twiddle your thumbs if you wish. That's right! —It's the human thumb. Sure, other animals have wings, hooves, and fins. And some, like apes and chimpanzees, have small thumbs. But only humans have a really good version of what are called **opposable** thumbs.

Opposable means that human thumbs can be opposite human fingers. Try it—touch each of your fingertips to your thumb tip. Simple, right? But this is very special in the world of animals. Because the human thumb is opposable, we can pick up, hold, and handle things. Other animals cannot do that (except, sort of, our nearest and dearest relatives—apes and chimpanzees).

Life as we know it happened because humans could use their opposable thumbs to farm, hunt, handle basic tools, build machines, and write. The things that other animals have—like wings, hooves, and fins—aren't much good for this farming, building, and writing stuff.

Along with the brain, it's the thumb that makes humans so different from other animals.

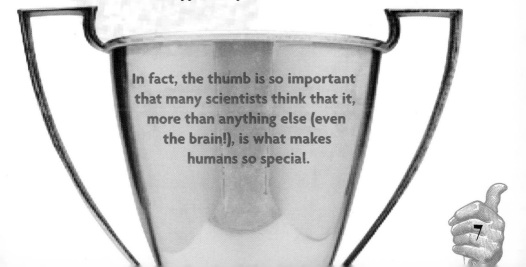

In fact, the thumb is so important that many scientists think that it, more than anything else (even the brain!), is what makes humans so special.

7

Think Clearly: A Top Ten List

1 Before you do anything else, even before you go to the bathroom, **figure out what your project is.** Is it a group project? A written report? Two pages or five pages? Oral? Two minutes or five minutes?

2 **What do you have to do?** If you're working in a group, figure out what you have to do. (Even though it might not always seem like it, teachers know who the real slackers are in any group.)

3 Get started so you can get finished. Don't wait to start! You might get sick. You might get invited to a party. Stuff like this really happens.

 Research: Allow five days, one hour per day.

 Writing: For a **written** report , write two hours the first day. On the second day, re-write (make it better!) for one hour. Take the next day off (you deserve it!). Re-write for 30 minutes on the fourth day.

Practice: For an **oral** project , practice your presentation for three days. On the first day, practice it out loud behind closed doors two times, and once with a parent. On the second day, practice it once—with any changes from your parent—behind closed doors; once more for a parent; and one more time behind closed doors. On the third day, practice it one last time in private.

👍 *An* **exhibit**  should be finished two days before it is due to school. Ask family members to check it out for a day. Any problems with it? Tape coming off? Anything breaking? This leaves you *one* day to fix it.

4 **Check the spelling on all written materials.**

5 **Has somebody, like a family member, checked over all your materials?** Sometimes a different set of eyes sees stuff you don't.

6 **Presenting tomorrow?** Get a good night's rest.

7 **Look one last time at your teacher's instructions.** Have you done everything?

8 Pack the night before. Is your exhibit big fragile? Have you figured out a way to get school without wrecking it? Don't wait bus is outside honking its horn to fig' packing stuff.

9 If you can, pee before class.

10 **Your contribution to this Top Ten List (whatever we forgot):**

_____ __

_____

_____

Getting Started
(The Amazing Note Card)

For as long as you are a student, you'll be doing school projects.

For every project you must do one thing: collect information (also known as **research**). That's what a school project is all about: collecting information and presenting it to somebody. That somebody may be a teacher or other students.

So how do you collect all that information? With the amazing note card.

The Amazing Note Card

You can collect information about the thumb, for example, by **finding** a book (like this one), a magazine, or a newspaper; or **watching** a video or TV show; or **searching** the Internet; or **interviewing** somebody (see page 62).

Whenever you find something interesting on your topic, write it down on a note card. Be sure to write on the card where you found the information (for example: **Our Friend the Thumb**, a book by Joe Hitchhiker,

school library). Keep creating these cards until you have
a stack of them.

You've done all your research? **Great!** Now arrange the
cards in some order that makes sense.
For example, cards on the same topic
should be together. One card should
follow another for good reason.

Imagine that if you taped all the cards
together, like a string of cut-out dolls,
you'd have a very rough first draft of a
paper or presentation. **Neat, eh?**

On the next 13 pages are 44 note card-like pieces of
information to get you started.

Read through some of them. Go ahead, right now. (We'll wait.)

See how they don't read like a normal book or paper?
That's because these note cards are just the beginning of
your work. They are not yet in an order that makes any
sense. They're still like a bunch of letters (B, H, M, T, U)
that have to be put in order so that they make up a word
(THUMB).

For example, if you just copied these note cards out of the
book and handed them to your teacher, the teacher would
say something like, "That's a good start. NOW FINISH
IT! Go write a paper that makes sense. These are just
stones. Build a wall with them."

If this is a group project, think about how to share this note card work. By topic is a good way. One person may research other animals' "hands" (paws, wings, etc.) to show how human hands and thumbs are different. Someone else may do evolution—what else besides our thumbs sets us apart from our nearest relatives, the great apes? Someone else may research the bones, muscles, and tendons of the human hand and thumb. Someone else may find all the "extra" weird stuff on fingerprints, thumb trivia, etc.

You can buy packs of note cards or cut paper into pieces about 3 inches high and 5 inches wide (use this paragraph's note card as a guide). Keep your note cards together with a paper clip, or, if you do a lot of research, a rubber band will work.

Really Helpful Hint:
Once you have a lot of note cards, you should figure out what information is really important, what is somewhat important, and what is not important at all. So review all your note cards and mark those that contain really important information. For example, over the next few pages we've marked those note cards that contain the really important information with an exclamation mark:

And, hey, good luck with your note cards!

1

People used to think that an itchy thumb was a sign that the person would soon have a visitor.

2

An easy way to remember which hand is your left and which is your right, is to hold your hands—palms open but fingers together—in front of you. Now lower your thumbs so that they are pointing at each other. The thumb and finger that create an "L" are on your Left hand.

fido

3

Some people believe that people with long thumbs are stubborn and those with wide thumbs are, or will be, wealthy.

Dog thumb

4!
The most important thing about the human thumb is that it is opposable. Opposable means that the tip of your thumb can touch the tip of each of your fingers. Because of your <u>opposable</u> thumb, you can hold and pick up things. Other animals either cannot do that (dog) or do it well (monkey).

5!
  Because of the opposable thumb, humans can pick up, hold, and use simple tools. Although the gorilla and chimpanzee have opposable thumbs, their thumbs are much shorter than ours. They can use simple "tools"—like a hollow blade of grass to suck up grubs. But they cannot make a "straw" from a piece of paper.

6!
Imagine if your thumb and fingers were like your big toe and your other toes. Go ahead, wiggle your toes! Now imagine trying to bake a cake, bat a ball, drive a go-cart, play tennis, write a secret note, or get dressed with your toes. It simply wouldn't work.

Monkey thumb

7!

Of all mammals, the human's thumb is farthest from its fellow fingers. This lets the human thumb move all by itself without the fingers moving.

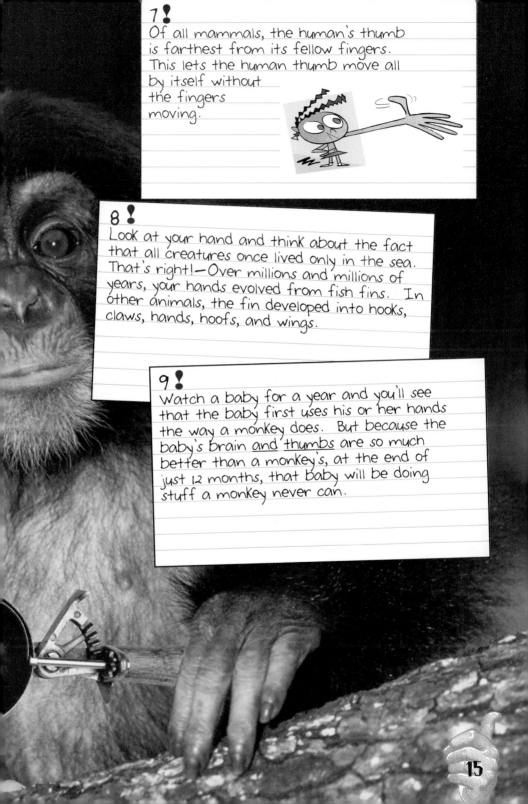

8!

Look at your hand and think about the fact that all creatures once lived only in the sea. That's right!—Over millions and millions of years, your hands evolved from fish fins. In other animals, the fin developed into hooks, claws, hands, hoofs, and wings.

9!

Watch a baby for a year and you'll see that the baby first uses his or her hands the way a monkey does. But because the baby's brain and thumbs are so much better than a monkey's, at the end of just 12 months, that baby will be doing stuff a monkey never can.

10

Sucking a thumb is about the first thing anybody does. Babies, when still inside of their mothers before being born, suck on their thumbs. This thumb-sucking prepares kids to suck milk once they've entered the outside world.

11

Thumb-sucking does not cause buck teeth. Some scientists think that thumb-sucking may help the muscles and bones of the face to develop.

WOW! NICE FACIAL BONE STRUCTURE!

OBVIOUSLY A CHILDHOOD THUMB-SUCKER!

12

Regardless of buck teeth or no buck teeth, thumb-sucking is not very healthy. When somebody with a cold sneezes, germs that ride out on the sneeze live for about three hours. If your thumb touches wherever those germs land and then you suck your thumb, you can get sick.

13 Most fingers have three bones, called phalanges (one is called a phalanx). Now, look at a non-thumb finger. Ready? Count! One bone goes from the hand to the first knuckle. A second bone goes from knuckle to knuckle. And a third bone goes from knuckle to fingertip (see drawing, page 52). The wonderful thumb has only two bones and one knuckle.

14
The thumb moves in mysterious ways. It can bend, straighten, move forward or backward, and even rotate across the palm. Your fingers cannot move as much as your thumb. Go ahead, move them around. Check it out!

15
Gloves are to keep your thumbs, fingers, and hands warm, right? Maybe. It depends upon <u>who</u> you are and <u>when</u> you are. In the Middle Ages (the years 500 through 1450), a man would show his love to a fair maiden (girlfriend) by pinning one of her gloves to his chest clothing.

like so. . .

16 If you ever have the chance, watch a chipmunk (or squirrel) sit and eat a nut. The chipmunk needs both paws to hold the nut to its mouth. Yet because of the opposable thumb, as a human kid you can hold a nut with one hand and this book with another. You can also, at the same time, carry the nut, walk into another room, <u>and</u> talk on a portable phone. Not the chipmunk. Like other animals, the chipmunk must use its mouth to hold and carry. Think about a life in which you have to carry everything in your mouth.

17 ❗

Animals use their paws to travel, even a few inches. People use their feet. Even the hands of chimpanzees, with their little thumbs, are really designed for getting around from branch to branch. Even raccoons can hang from trees with their tiny thumbs!

18

About three and a half months before you were born, tiny ridges formed on your fingers and toes. Although those ridges grew larger, the pattern they formed will never change. No two people, not even identical twins, have the same pattern. These patterns are fingerprints.

Raccoon thumb

19

What's in the fingerprint left behind by a robber? Water, salt, fat, oil, and chemicals—stuff that is always leaking out of our bodies and onto our skin. What's neat is that the more nervous the burglar is, the more of that stuff leaks out, which makes for more obvious fingerprints.

20

If a burglar takes off his shoes so that he can put his socks on over his hands so that he won't leave any fingerprints, oops!—he'll leave toe prints.

21

England first set up a fingerprinting system to identify criminals in 1900. The United States FBI (Federal Bureau of Investigation) did likewise in 1924. The FBI now has over 200 million prints on file.

THiS ONE'S MY PERSONAL FAVORITE!

PRINT #
3,692,783

22

There are three types of fingerprints. Visible prints are those that can be seen because the person who left them had dirty fingers. Plastic prints are those that leave an impression in something, like food or paint. Latent prints are invisible.

23

For latent prints to be seen, a light powder is dusted in the area. The powder clings to the oils left behind by the finger. The fingerprint pattern can then be seen.

24

NOW WE CAN CATCH **BAD GUYS** IN A SPLIT SECOND!

A fingerprint-identification system on a computer can scan and review 500 to 1,200 prints per second. What such a computer does in 45 seconds would take a person 17,000 hours.

25

Your thumb bends and moves because of its joints. A joint is where two bones meet. There's fluid in the joint and tissue (cartilage) on the ends of the bones to keep two bones from rubbing against each other. The fluid doesn't leak away because the joint sits in a bag made of body tissue.

26 ‼

But what makes all the parts of your hand, including the thumb, move? Muscles. Relax your hand. Look at the underside of your lower arm. Now make a tight fist. See stuff move under your skin? Those are the muscles—called flexors—that pull your hand into a fist.

27 ‼

Make another tight fist. Turn your arm over so you're looking at the hairy top of it. Now open your hand and stretch it out. See that movement under the skin of your hand? Do it again. Watch closely. Those are the extensors, the muscles that open and stretch your hand, at work.

28 !

Tendons are like small ropes or strings of tissue that run from the muscles to the finger bones. Tendons carry the power of your muscles to the bones. Tap your fingers on a table (as if pretending to play the piano). You can see the tendons move on the back of your hand. (Or if you're a bear, try holding on to a tree trunk).

29 !

The thumb is the most important and busiest of your fingers. The thumb does about half of all the hand's work.

HEY! I'M GETTING TIRED OF ALWAYS DOING THE PINKY'S WORK!

30

What do people do if they are born without a thumb or lose a thumb in an accident? Surgeons can move a finger—or even a toe—into the thumb position. A hand with three fingers and a finger-ish or toe-ish thumb may first look a bit strange. But it will <u>work</u> like a thumb, which is great!

31

Thumbs work all day and usually lead the way into most any activity. Often their work is dangerous (more surgical repairs are performed on the hand than on any other part of the body). Luckily, fingers carry around some great protection with them—their nails.

32

The thumbnail is almost as wonderful as the thumb. You can scratch an itch with fingernails, you can decorate them, you can open things with them, and, unlike the claws of poor animals, your nails lie flat and don't get in the way when you pick up things.

PICASSO, EAT YOUR HEART OUT!

33

The crescent white part at the base of your nail is the lunula (commonly called the moon). The bigger the lunula, the faster the nail is growing. Look at your fingers. It's probably your good old thumb that has the biggest lunula. The thumbnail is your fastest growing fingernail.

34

Your nails can tell your doctor a lot about your health. For example, pneumonia will slow nail growth. And nails that break or crack easily may indicate a poor diet.

squirrel
thumb

35!

The skin of your fingertips sticks out further than your finger bones. If it wasn't for the nails, your fingertip skin would just flimsily bend backward whenever you tried to pick up something. For example, put on a glove, but don't put your index finger in all the way. Now try to pick up something with your thumb and index finger. See? A flimsy fingertip would be a problem.

36

If someone's good at growing plants, people like to say that the person has a "green thumb".

37

Sir Isaac Newton once said that he didn't need any further proof of God's existence than the wonderful human thumb.

38

Isaac Newton was born in 1642 and died in 1727. He was an English physicist and mathematician who thought very highly of his thumb, discovered how gravity works, and determined that light is composed of many colors.

39

The friendly custom of extending an open hand to shake hands is a gesture from the earliest of human history to show that no weapon is being carried.

40 ❗

An ape's or monkey's thumb is less developed than a human's thumb. Because of this, the ape's or monkey's grip—although it may be strong—is inefficient. Think of the animal grip as a "power" grip and your hand as a "precision" grip. For example, you can shuffle a deck of cards and play "Go Fish" but a monkey can't do that. On the other hand, a monkey can very easily hang from a limb for hours but you can't do that.

41

When it's time for babies to do something with their thumbs other than suck them, what are they to do? Use their toes to train their thumbs. A kid uses a thumb and a finger to grab a toe, let go, grab another toe, let go, and so on and so on, day after day.

baby thumb

42

In Scotland, agreements were once sealed with thumbs. Both people licked their thumbs and then pressed their wet thumbs together. This seal was taken very seriously. (It wasn't something to thumb your nose at!)

43 ❗

The human is the only animal who always walks upright, on the feet, so that the hands are totally free to do all kinds of things. This makes us very special in the world of animals.

44

In 1972, the unstaffed space ship, <u>Pioneer 10</u>, was sent into space. Its purpose was to travel beyond our solar system (even beyond the planet of Pluto!) and enter interstellar (among the stars) space.
Should <u>Pioneer 10</u> meet up with other intelligent life, the greeting here was included. See how the opposable thumb is given big play?

Getting Your Dexters in a Row
(Setting Your Priorities)

Well, What About the Thumb?

For your science project, are you going to present everything there is to know about thumbs? Or are you going to focus on the opposable thumb? Or on how animal claws and hooves are different from human hands and thumbs?

You've done some research by this point. What part of that information are you going to use? Or do you need to do more research, maybe into specific thumb issues?

Sample

Let's say you decided to focus your thumb science project on the human thumb and how it is like, or not like, what animals have at the ends of their arms. Go back to the note cards. Although the ones in this book are only a sampling, pretend they are *all* your note cards. Now mark those—go ahead, use a pencil, put a little check mark (✓) on each one—that you would use to prepare a short oral or written presentation. Remember your thumb topic is "The Human Thumb versus What Animals Are Stuck With."

To check your selection against ours, see page 64.

Organizing All the Information

Be very clear as to what your presentation is about. You do this by giving a title to your exhibit , or with the opening sentences of a paper , or in the first few sentences of an oral report

26

This will be helpful to your listeners and readers. But, more important, a clear understanding of what you're working on will be of great help to you. Let's pretend your presentation topic is "The Differences Between a Human Thumb and a Monkey Thumb." You might want to write that down on a piece of paper and keep it in front of you.

Remember, in a paper or oral presentation, first clearly write what your topic is. Follow that with a presentation of the information you collected and selected. At the end, write your topic again in a summary.

Really Helpful Hints:

☞ This is a science project. Do not use goofy humor, superstitions, or rumors as your main topic. At most, this kind of information should be given to pep up a report. A little goes a long way. Remember, your science teacher is looking for scientific information.

☞ Once you've picked the note cards from which you'll write a presentation, number them! Otherwise, dropping them might be a full-blown disaster.

☞ If you're doing an oral presentation and using note cards or sheets of paper, number them! That way, you won't worry about losing your place when you're in front of the class.

☞ If you will refer to a written paper during your oral presentation, make doing that as easy as possible. Print out the presentation in large, easy-to-read letters

LIKE THIS.

27

THUMB-THINGS
(Experiments and Activities)

Discover the Thumb

For an oral report to your classmates, the short paragraph and four little activities that follow are a fun beginning. What you can say is *italicized*.

> *"Stop, pause, and discover your thumb."* (Hold your thumb high.) *"The thumb is always there."* (Look at your raised thumb.) *"It is often used but easily ignored. Let's stop for a moment to rediscover our thumbs."*

(Instruct your classmates.)

"Hold your hands up. Come on, up high!" (Do this along with your classmates.) *"What's the thickest finger on your hand?"*

"Stretch your hands, point them toward the sky." (Do it.) *"See that? When your fingers point up and down, your thumbs can point side to side."*

"Using any one finger—but not the thumb—on one hand, touch the other fingers of the same hand." (Do it.) *"Is it easy? How about when your pinky tries to touch the middle fingers? Now do the same with the thumb. Easiest of all?"*

"Put your arms out to your sides so that your fingers are pointing side to side." (Do it.) *"Now your thumbs can point up and down."* (Do it.)

Now you can go on to explain how special and important the opposable thumb is. This is information that you gathered in your research (including information in the Sample Research section of this book, pages 13 – 25).

29

The Secret Life of the Thumb

 For an oral presentation, "The Secret Life of the Thumb" is a way to have fun while showing how important the thumb is.

Be **sure** to have a roll of adhesive tape.

Begin by saying something like:

"Not sure what your thumb does all day? There's a great way to find out—don't use it!"

Ask for a volunteer. Have the volunteer write, as neatly as possible, his or her name on the chalkboard. Now tape the volunteer's thumb to his or her hand. (Be sure to tape the **writing** hand.) Have the volunteer write on the chalkboard again. The handwriting will probably be awful.

 Ask for another volunteer. Have this volunteer unbutton and re-button something. Next tape both of the volunteer's thumbs to his or her hand. Now, have the volunteer unbutton and re-button again.

This should be fun.

Ask for more volunteers to perform simple, everyday tasks. First they do an activity with the thumb, and then without the thumb. Try tying shoes, turning pages, shuffling cards, picking up a dime, throwing and catching a ball, shaking hands, drinking a glass of water, opening a door, and eating a cookie.

You could end your presentation by saying something like:

"Get the idea? Your thumb is very important. Most people take all the credit for playing and learning and the poor thumb gets no credit at all. If I ever win one of those big awards on TV—like the Academy Awards, where people thank teachers, parents, and friends—I'll be the first celebrity to thank my thumb."

The length of this presentation is really up to you and your teacher. You can use 2 volunteers or 20. For a more complete version of "The Secret Life of the Thumb," see "The Thumbless Obstacle Course" on pages 34 – 37.

Helpful Hint:

For a group project, one member can do the presentation and ask for volunteers. Another can tape the volunteers' thumbs. And another can be responsible for supplies such as adhesive tape, a piece of clothing with a button, shoes with shoelaces, a ball, cookies, and whatever else your group wishes to test.

Thumbprinting

Here's an easy way to take a thumbprint. This activity can be part of your own  or a group's presentation . It could also be an illustration for a written report .

 1 Using a pencil, make a black smudgy patch on a piece of paper.

 2 Rub the tip of your thumb over the patch until it is black and smudgy.

 3 Stick a piece of clear adhesive tape over the tip of your thumb. Firmly press down on the tape to be sure that it sticks.

4 Lift the tape off your thumb, and the black thumbprint will come off with it.

 5 Stick the tape onto a piece of white paper. You now have a real thumbprint. Note on the paper whose thumb the print comes from.

JOEY SMITH
LEFT THUMB
9/2000

Compare the thumbprint with the information on page 42 ("You, and Only You!"). Is the thumbprint of the arch, loop, or whorl style?

Thumbprinting is also a great exhibit activity. Try something like this:

Place instructions like those on page 32 (steps 1 through 5) on poster board.

Place thumbprint style information (see page 42) on poster board.

Place poster board on table.

Place several pencils and rolls of tape on table.

Place a Thumbprinting Research Chart on the table (see below). Start the fun by taping on your own thumbprint, writing in your name, and identifying your own thumbprint style.

Thumbprinting Research Chart

Tape Your Thumbprint Here	Name	Arch, Loop, or Whorl
	Dexter	Loop

The Thumbless Obstacle Course

 Place the following items on a table:

- piece of clothing with a zipper
- an empty *plastic* soda bottle with a screw-on top
- tennis or rubber ball
- piece of clothing with a button
- chalk

Write the following chart on the chalkboard:

The Thumbless Obstacle Course

Name	Time with thumbs	Time without thumbs
_____	_____	_____
_____	_____	_____
_____	_____	_____
_____	_____	_____
_____	_____	_____
_____	_____	_____

Be sure to have a watch with a second hand for your teacher, and let your teacher know what to expect!

Ask for a volunteer from the class. Have the volunteer write his or her name on the chart. Explain to the volunteer and class that your teacher will time the volunteer as he or she, as quickly as possible, completes all of the tasks on the table. Like this:

 open and close the zipper

 take the lid off the soda bottle and screw it back on

 throw the ball to you, catch the ball back from you

 tie the shoelaces

 button and unbutton the button

write his or her name on the chalkboard

As an example, you should do the obstacle course first. Have the teacher be the one to play catch with you.

OK, have the volunteer do the obstacle course. Write his or her name on the chalkboard chart and write the time it took for the volunteer to finish the obstacle course in the "time with thumb" column. **Now tape the volunteer's thumbs to his or her hands, so that the thumbs really can't be used.** Have the volunteer do the obstacle course again. Enter how long it takes in the "time without thumbs" column. It should take **much** longer to do the course without a thumb.

Do as many volunteers as your teacher permits or you have time for.

In the end, compare the time "with thumbs" and the time "without thumbs" and point out what you will have already proven—that the thumb is really important!

The Thumbless Obstacle Course is a great group activity. One person can get the stuff for the table. Instead of the teacher, another person can do the timing. Another can write information on the chart. And another can first complete the obstacle course to demonstrate the activity.

For a class presentation by yourself, see "The Secret Life of the Thumb" on page 30 for an easier version of these activities.

The Manual Alphabet

Imagine not being able to hear or speak.

Maybe this takes very little imagination. Maybe you're hearing impaired or know people who are. Do you or they use sign language? If so, imagine not having thumbs and trying to use sign language.

The thumb is a very important thing. Not just to thumb-suckers and ballplayers, but especially to those who use the Manual Alphabet to communicate. Give it a try. See if you can learn the Manual Alphabet (on page 57).

The Manual Alphabet is a good thing to work into a thumb presentation. For example, make copies of page 57. At the end of your thumb presentation, hand out the copies. Tell your classmates to watch you carefully. Spell out something for them, like "O-U-R F-R-I-E-N-D T-H-E- T-H-U-M-B" or your teacher's name ("M-R N-E-W-T-O-N"). Whoever gets the message first wins. (A candy bar or cookie? That's cool.) Use this moment to remind your audience how important the thumb is to **everybody**.

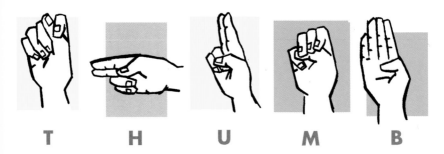

T   H   U   M   B

Rules of Thumb

> "A rule of thumb is a homemade recipe for making a guess. It is an easy-to-remember guide that falls somewhere between a mathematical formula and a shot in the dark. A farmer, for instance, knows to plant his corn when oak leaves are the size of squirrels' ears. Rules of thumb are a kind of tool. They help you think through a problem."

— *Tom Parker (author, Rules of Thumb)*

There are thousands of rules of thumb. For example, as a rule of thumb:

👍 The number of guests at a child's birthday party should equal the child's age (for a third birthday, invite three guests; for a sixth birthday, invite six; and so on).

👍 When cooking spaghetti, you'll know it's done when you throw it at the wall and it sticks.

👍 One ostrich egg will serve 24 people for brunch.

👍 A child is old enough to send to school when he can cross his arms over his head and grasp his ears with his opposite hand. (Have the class try this one. Are they old enough to be in school?)

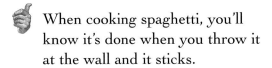

👍 You should expect to lose one sock every time you do your laundry.

Can you think of any? See if others in your class can. Write them on the chalkboard.

Mystery Theater

Mysteries of the thumb, hand, and fingers are easily solved once you understand the hand's tendons.

Tendons are cords of tissue that run from the muscles to the finger bones. Tendons carry the power of your muscles to your bones. Tap your fingers on a table, as if you're playing the piano. Did you see the tendons move on the back of your hand? (Have everybody in class try these activities.) Or, straighten your hand and then bend your fingers back as far as you can. Did you see the tendons stand out on the back of your hand?

The ring finger shares a tendon with the middle finger. That's why it is so hard to move the ring finger without moving the middle finger. You can demonstrate this with three exercises.

1 Place your hand on a table with your middle finger tucked under your hand. You can lift your thumb, right? And the index and little finger, right? But because the ring finger and the middle finger share a tendon, the ring finger is stuck. It can't lift when the middle finger is pulling down because a tendon can't pull in two different ways!

2 Ask a volunteer to put her hand out, palm up, with her ring finger in toward the palm of her hand, like this. Now flip the tip of her ring finger a bit. Does her ring finger wiggle uncontrollably? For many people it does. Because the middle and ring fingers share a tendon and the middle finger is extended straight, the muscle that controls the tip of the ring finger is having difficulty doing its job. Try this activity on yourself. Do you get the uncontrollable wiggling?

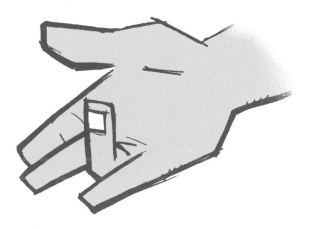

3 Hold your hands together, finger to finger but palms not touching. Try moving the thumbs and fingers apart, one at a time. No problem, right? Now bend your middle fingers in so that the lower knuckle of each is touching the other, like this. Try again to move the thumbs and fingers apart, one at a time. How did it go with the ring finger? Not well, right? It's that shared tendon again.

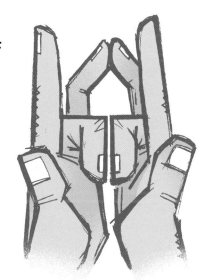

You, and Only You!

First, get a magnifying glass (among the teachers in your school, you should be able to find at least one).

This is a great group activity for three or four classmates. They're going to use the magnifying glass to study each other's thumbs.

Check out those thumbs! Do any of them have hairs on the fronts or backs of their thumbs? Do you see the small pores through which sweat and oil leak onto your skin? Be sure to notice the skin's pattern of ridges, separated by valleys. This pattern is the thumbprint.

Now stop! Pause! Be wowed! —the thumbprint now being looked at is so unique that only one other person will have that same print within the next 466,037,700 years. Thumb-mazing!

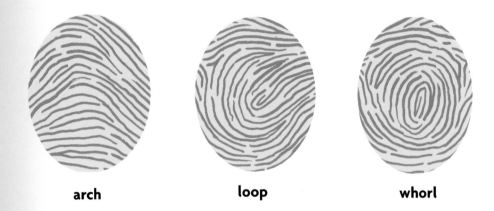

arch   loop   whorl

An **arch**, a **loop**, and a **whorl** are the three basic thumbprint patterns. Combinations of these patterns are called **composites**.

Have your classmates identify each other's print patterns. Note on a chart, like the one below, the student's name and fingerprint pattern. Which is the most common? Do boys or girls have a certain pattern? Do brunettes or blondes have a certain pattern? Do you have twins in your class? Do they share a similar pattern?

Student's Name	Arch	Loop	Whorl	Composite
_____	_____	_____	_____	_____
_____	_____	_____	_____	_____
_____	_____	_____	_____	_____
_____	_____	_____	_____	_____
_____	_____	_____	_____	_____
_____	_____	_____	_____	_____
_____	_____	_____	_____	_____
_____	_____	_____	_____	_____
_____	_____	_____	_____	_____

more ➤→

This is also a great exhibit activity. Create a poster to be placed on an exhibit table. Title the poster *"You, and Only You!"* Include on the poster a paragraph or two about what fingerprints are and their importance. Also include the name—and a simple sketch—of each of the basic fingerprint patterns.

Your exhibit should ask people to look at their thumbs with the magnifying glass and then complete a chart, like the one on the previous page. Put information about your own thumb in the first row of the chart. That way people will understand what to do. Use a string to tie a pencil and the magnifying glass to the table. (It's easy for forgetful people to walk away with the pencil or glass.)

Check your chart after the exhibit. What have you learned? Are there any patterns to the thumbprint patterns?

PosterBody

Here's a neat idea. Pretend it's the night before a class report is due. Time is running out, and—oh no!—you can't find any poster board and it's too late to go out and buy some. BUT!—in your home is a non-toxic marker that a parent* will permit you to use on your skin.

So use your body as your poster! Seriously. Instead of doing drawings of a hand and labeling it on a poster, you're going to label your actual hand. You may have to have a parent or responsible brother or sister help with the lettering.

Below are samples of what you can label.

It's also good to show what some of those labeled parts do. Point to your *flexor* muscle and then make a fist. Your classmates should see it move. Turn your arm over and point to the *extensor* muscle. Open your hand, stretch it out. Your classmates may be able to see it move too.

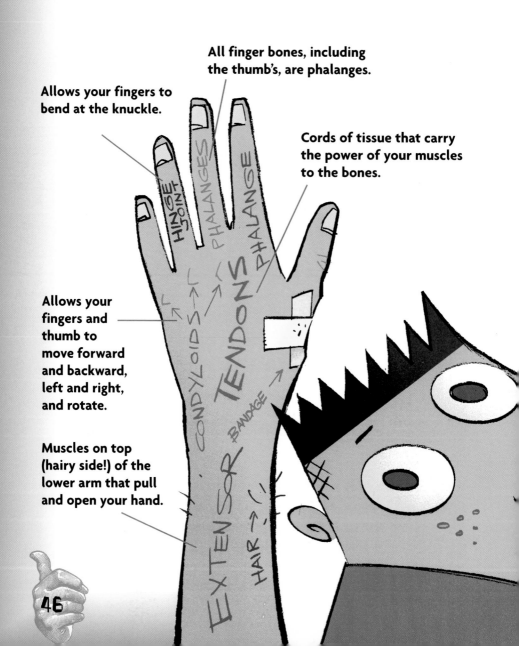

All finger bones, including the thumb's, are phalanges.

Allows your fingers to bend at the knuckle.

Cords of tissue that carry the power of your muscles to the bones.

Allows your fingers and thumb to move forward and backward, left and right, and rotate.

Muscles on top (hairy side!) of the lower arm that pull and open your hand.

HINGE JOINT

PHALANGES

PHALANGE

CONDYLOIDS

TENDONS

BANDAGE

EXTENSOR

HAIR

Show the back of your hand, where the tendon is labeled. Now pretend to play the piano in the air. Your classmates should see it move as well.

With **PosterBody** you can wow your teacher and classmates, write all over your skin, and save $1.50 in poster board costs. This is a very rare opportunity.

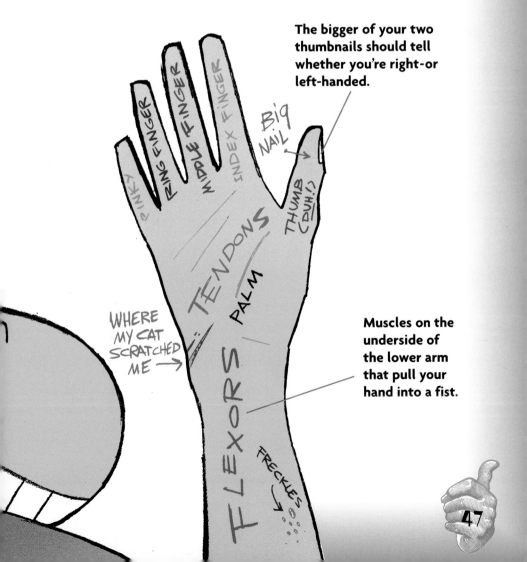

The bigger of your two thumbnails should tell whether you're right-or left-handed.

Muscles on the underside of the lower arm that pull your hand into a fist.

47

Assorted Thumbgoofing

At the beginning or end of an oral report, it's sometimes fun to have your classmates goof off a little bit. Here are five simple and fun goofings.

1 Quick! Fold your hands! Which thumb lies on top? If you're a lefty, it's supposedly the right thumb. Vice-versa if you're right-handed. Does this really work? Some people think so. Some people doubt it. Did it work in your class?

2 See who in your class can do the following.

3 Find a piece of cardboard, at least 6 inches by 6 inches. Cut two holes in the middle of the cardboard. (Use a penny to trace with.) Leave a penny-sized space in between the two holes. This will be your thumb wrestling mat. Have two classmates lock fingers under the mat, stick their thumbs up through the two holes, and the match is on.

To make a really cool wrestling mat, decorate the cardboard. Create and include a "ThumbMania" logo!

Pretend this is the **World Federation of Thumb Wrestling**! Name your thumbs. Instead of Hulk Hogan how about Thulk Thumb? Or Punky Pinky? And if your name is Thomas, you've just got to be Tom Thumb.

May the best thumb win!

4 One way to tell if you're left-handed or right-handed is to look at your thumbnails. The thumbnail on your favored hand is wider. Does this really work? Does it work for your classmates?

5 Use your thumb like a ruler and measure the following:

1. How high is your ear, from its bottom to its top?

2. How far is it from the tip of your nose to your eyebrows?

3. How far is it from the middle of your face (between the eyebrows) to the outer corner of your eye?

4. How far is it between the tip of your nose and your chin?

5. How far is it between your eyebrows and your hairline?

"One thumb" is the answer in each case. **Weird, isn't it?** It's as if your thumb was made first, and then used to design your face and head.

Really Helpful Stuff!

These next six pages are here for you to use as you wish. That's right! — Just go ahead and trace or photocopy these pages. You can then glue or tape them into a written presentation, copy and distribute them to your classmates, or attach them to a poster. It's up to you.

Thumbprint Patterns

arch

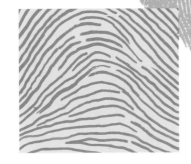

loop

whorl

Thumbprints that are combinations of these patterns are called **composites**.

Bones of the Human Hand

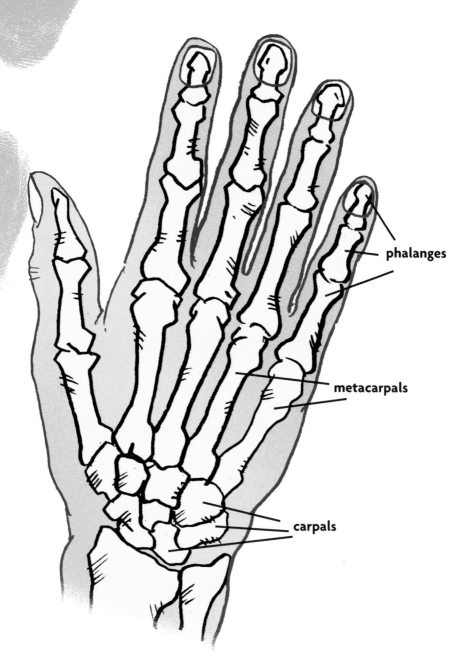

phalanges

metacarpals

carpals

Bones of Animal "Hands"

pig foot

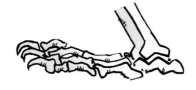

badger foot

seal

elephant foot

bat wing

cat paw

Muscles and Tendons of the Human Hand

**extensor muscles on the
back of the hand**

**flexor muscles on the
palm side of the hand**

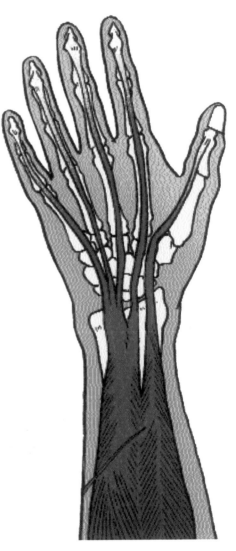

Animal Hands

human hand

duck foot

chimpanzee hand

bird wing

elephant hand

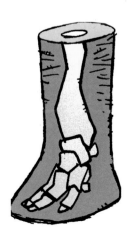

Joints of the Human Hand

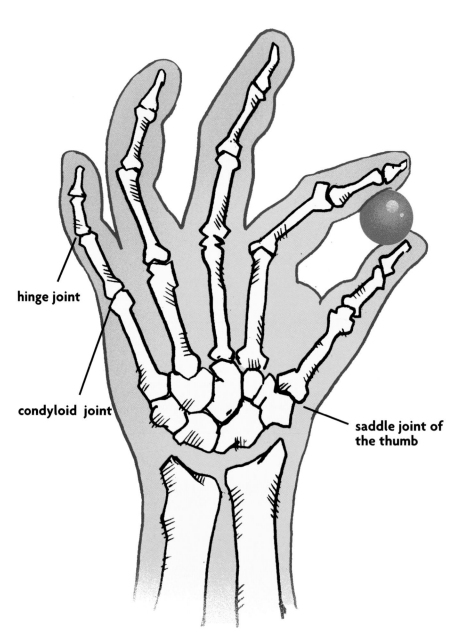

hinge joint

condyloid joint

saddle joint of
the thumb

The Manual Alphabet

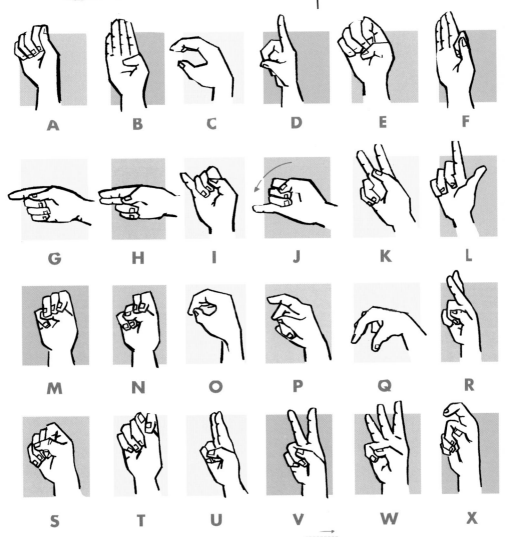

A B C D E F

G H I J K L

M N O P Q R

S T U V W X

Y Z

57

Sign Language

(selected words)

animal

game

baby

house
1.

2.

cat

drink

I love you

jump

eat

father

kiss

learn

mother

noon

out

play

quiet

read

scissors

tree

umbrella

walk

x-ray

you

zoo

FuN StuFf

 When doing an oral presentation, it's sometimes a good idea to have fun with your listeners. Doing this actually helps them to pay attention.

This kind of material is really not right for a written report.

Below is some amusing and informative stuff to drop into an oral presentation on the thumb:

 Thumbelina is a fictional character from literature who grew to be no bigger than a thumb. She traveled around on a leaf pulled by a butterfly.

 "Knock knock."

"Who's there?"

"Thumb."

"Thumb who?"

"Thumb fun we're having now."

 Tom Thumb is a fictional character who sneaked into people's pockets to steal stuff. His many adventures included being swallowed by a cow, a giant, and a fish.

 **To most of the world, a "thumbs up" sign means "OK." (You might mention here that when you're done with your presentation, you are hoping to get a "thumbs up.")**

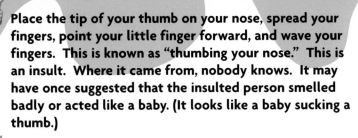 Place the tip of your thumb on your nose, spread your fingers, point your little finger forward, and wave your fingers. This is known as "thumbing your nose." This is an insult. Where it came from, nobody knows. It may have once suggested that the insulted person smelled badly or acted like a baby. (It looks like a baby sucking a thumb.)

Form a circle by bringing together the tip of your thumb and index finger. To most people this means "OK," "perfect," or "ready to go." But be careful!—in France this gesture is a symbol for zero. Waving it at somebody indicates that they are worthless.

Charles "General Tom Thumb" Stratton was a real person, born in 1838 to parents of normal size. However, Charles stopped growing at six months. In his teens, he was only two feet tall. As an adult, he grew to just a bit more than three feet (the length of a yardstick). In 1863 he married Lavinia Warren, who was 32 inches tall.

Really Helpful Hint:

Go back to the note cards on pages 13 to 25. Did you find some of them—like #1 and #3—more goofy than informative? These also can be used as a fun pause in your presentation. Ask if anyone has an itchy thumb. Tell them what people once thought that meant. Ask who has a long thumb. Tell them the superstition about long thumbs. Sometimes when you're doing research, you just don't know how you'll end up using the stuff you discover.

"Thumb" People to Interview

Ῠou will often learn more and have more fun interview-ing people than you will doing any other type of research. When *you* actually interview people instead of reading books and magazines *about* those people, they are calleed *primary sources*. (Helpful hint: teachers love it when you use primary sources.)

In researching the thumb, you may wish to interview a relative or family friend who lost a thumb in an accident (it does happen). You could also ask about the thumbs of the following people:

emergency medical technician

factory safety manager

guitar player

manicurist

physician

pianist

piano teacher

nurse

hand surgeon

thumb pianist

veterinarian

Thumb-thing Extra
(Additional Sources)

Following are some of the books we've discovered while learning about the thumb. Most are available at your school or public library. You and a helpful librarian are likely to find other books that we missed. When searching the library, keep key words like the following in mind: "hand," "thumb," "finger-printing," "knuckles," and "fingers."

Aliki. *My Hands*. New York: Thomas Y. Crowell, 1962.

Gryski, Camilla. *Hands On, Thumbs Up*. Reading, Massachusetts: Addison-Wesley Publishing Company, 1991.

Holub, Joan. *My First Book of Sign Language*. Mahwah, New Jersey: Troll Communications, 1996.

Jones, Charlotte Foltz. *Fingerprints and Talking Bones*. New York: Delacorte Press, 1997.

Parker, Tom. *Rules of Thumb*. Boston: Houghton Mifflin Company, 1983.

The Editors of Planet Dexter. *Lefty: A Handbook for Left-Handed Kids*. New York: Planet Dexter, 1997.

Silverstein, Alvin and Virginia. *The Story of Your Hand*. New York: G. P. Putnam's Sons, 1985.

Thomas, Peggy. *Talking Bones*. New York: Facts On File, 1995.

And while at the library . . .

Search beyond books. Check out the magazines, newspapers, videos, and microfilm catalogs.

Internet

Search keywords such as:

thumb
opposable
fingerprints
hand
finger

More No Sweat Science Projects!

Hairy Science

Hair-ily perfect for school science projects! With hair you can discover, experiment, and report on *genetics* (Will I be bald?), *zoology* (What do hair, feathers, and fur have in common?), *evolution* (Why do you take your head in for a haircut and not your foot or elbow?), and *anatomy* (What's the stuff made of?).

Shadowy Science

What are shadows? Why are they sometimes so big, sometimes so small, sometimes just the right size, and sometimes not there at all? How can shadows be used to tell time? Can there be shadows at night? Does a laser make a shadow? Great fun and great science, the shadow is a winning solution for most any science project.

Bouncing Science

Why are balls round and not square? What if they weren't? Why can you throw a baseball farther than a Ping-Pong ball but you can't throw a shot put farther than a baseball? Why can't you bowl on the beach? How do tennis players make the ball spin? How can a super ball bounce so high? Only science can answer these essential questions. This is the perfect subject for a *well-rounded* science project.

Suggestion Selection

(see "Getting Your Dexters in a Row," page 26)

If we were preparing a presentation of "The Human Thumb versus What Animals Are Stuck With," we would pull the following note cards out of those provided: 4, 5, 7, 8, 9, 10, 18, 19, 32, 40, 43. Then we would quickly get back on the Internet and to the library because we need at least another 20 note cards on this *specific* aspect of the thumb.